# INCREDIBLE

## ASIAN AMERICANS AND PACIFIC ISLANDERS
## WHO CHANGED THE WORLD

WRITTEN BY
OLYMPIC MEDALISTS

## MAIA AND ALEX
## SHIBUTANI

ILLUSTRATED BY

## DION MBD

VIKING

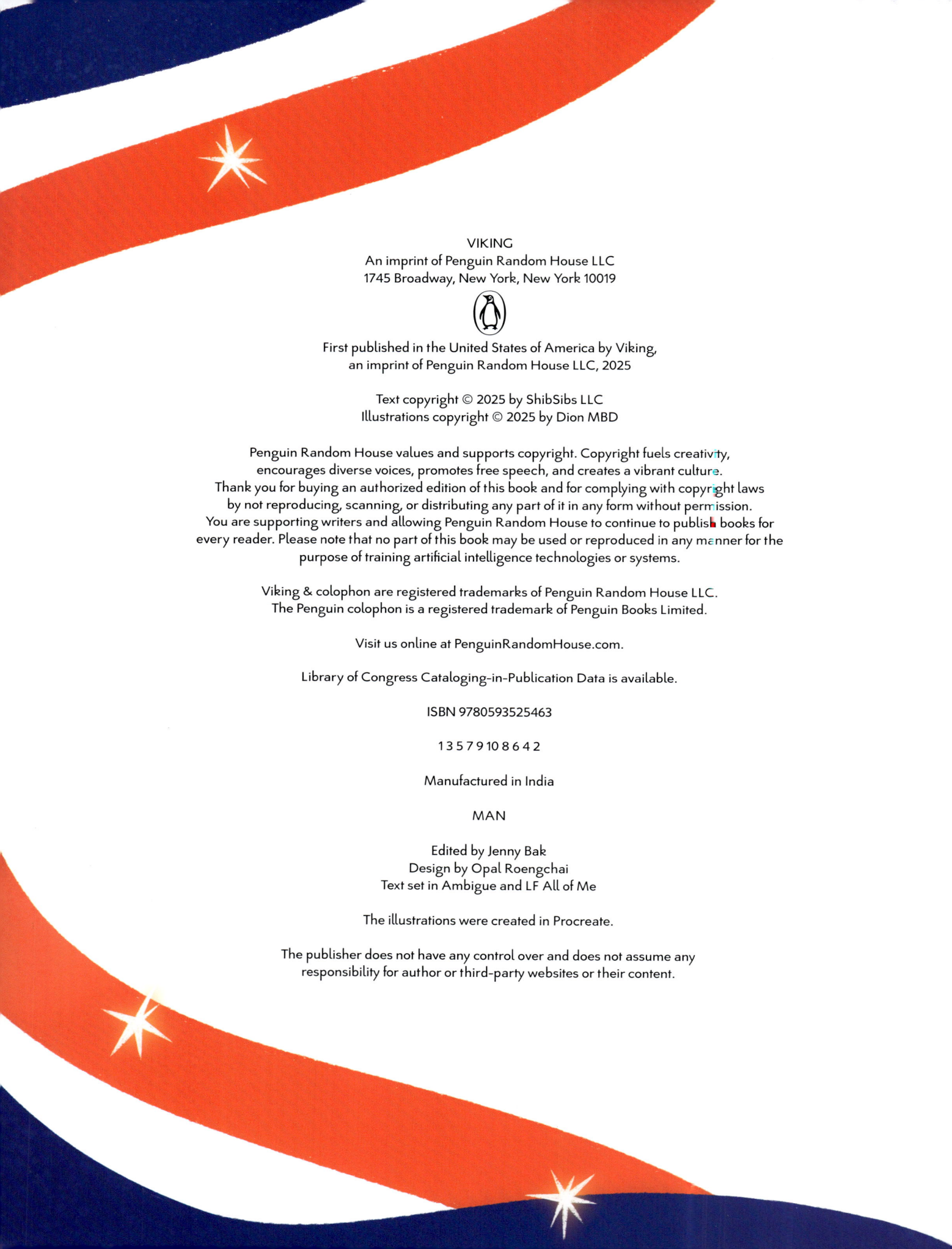

VIKING
An imprint of Penguin Random House LLC
1745 Broadway, New York, New York 10019

First published in the United States of America by Viking,
an imprint of Penguin Random House LLC, 2025

Visit us online at PenguinRandomHouse.com.

Library of Congress Cataloging-in-Publication Data is available.

ISBN 9780593525463

1 3 5 7 9 10 8 6 4 2

Manufactured in India

MAN

Edited by Jenny Bak
Design by Opal Roengchai
Text set in Ambigue and LF All of Me

The illustrations were created in Procreate.

To our readers of all ages . . .
Be inspired and live boldly.
Your dreams are possible!
—M. S. & A. S.

For Scarlett, my own incredible inspiration
—J. B. P.

For those who are underrepresented yet
continue to proudly embrace their heritage
—D. MBD

# KATHERINE SUI FUN CHEUNG

Looping and flipping across the California sky, Katherine was a daring biplane pilot. In the 1930s, she bravely challenged what people expected of a Chinese American mother by chasing her dreams to become the first Asian American aviatrix at the age of twenty-eight. Katherine's determination and soaring midair tricks opened up the skies for people around the world and inspired them to break barriers and reach new heights.

# DR. ISABELLA AIONA ABBOTT

Growing up in Hawai'i, Isabella first learned about "limu," or seaweed, from her mother and was so fascinated that she decided to become an expert in it. In 1950, she became the first Native Hawaiian woman to earn a PhD in science. Isabella was a pioneer in ethnobotany, the study of traditional plant uses by Native people. Her many years of research led to the discovery of hundreds of algae species. She shared her knowledge through her writing and teaching, as well as by baking delicious seaweed cakes for her friends.

# DR. NICOLE YAMASE

Nicole is a scientist from Micronesia who made history in 2021 when she boarded a submarine and became the first Pacific Islander to reach the Challenger Deep, the deepest known part of the ocean floor. On her ten-hour, nearly seven-mile journey, she brought a small model of a wooden canoe—a tribute to her navigator ancestors. Following her successful mission, Nicole expressed hope that Pacific Islander women will break more boundaries. "We belong on shore. We belong all the way at the bottom, and everywhere in between, too."

# DR. DALIP SINGH SAUND

Dalip grew up in British-controlled Punjab, India, before coming to America in the 1920s for school. He earned a PhD in mathematics, but his experiences with injustice in India and as a farmer in California during the Great Depression rallied him to become a civil rights leader and judge. After supporting American citizenship for Indians, he overcame ignorance and racism and was elected to the House of Representatives in 1956. As the first Asian American and Sikh congressman, Dalip is remembered as a trailblazer who believed in the power of democracy and diplomacy to change the world.

# PATSY MINK

Patsy, a third-generation Japanese American, was born on the island of Maui in 1927. She faced many forms of discrimination throughout her life but always found ways to make a difference. In 1964, Patsy was the first woman of color to be elected to Congress and would later become the first Asian American woman to run for president. One of her greatest triumphs was her work in creating Title IX, a law that supports equality and educational reform. Patsy is honored on the US quarter in recognition of her devotion to championing the rights of women, children, and minorities.

# TYRUS WONG

In 1920, young Tyrus and his father managed to immigrate to America during the Chinese Exclusion Act era, when most Chinese people weren't allowed in. Tyrus showed talent as an artist, but since his family couldn't afford supplies, he painted with water on newspapers. Tyrus's hard work earned him a scholarship to art school, and as an adult, his sketches and art style directly influenced the creative design for the movie *Bambi*. Later in his life, he was named a Disney Legend for his contributions. He's now recognized as one of the greatest multidisciplinary artists of his generation.

# PETER SOHN

Born in New York City to Korean immigrants, Pete is an artist who has also worked as a director, writer, animator, and voice actor on many movies. He is the inspiration behind the lovable Boy Scout Russell in *Up*, and he performs the voices of Emile, the always-hungry rat in *Ratatouille*, and Sox, the sweet robotic kitten in *Lightyear*. Pete is also the director of Pixar's Academy Award–nominated film *Elemental*. That story, about immigrants and boundary-crossing love, is deeply connected to his own childhood and family experiences.

# RONNIE DEL CARMEN

Ronnie grew up in the Philippines and immigrated to America as an adult following the peaceful People Power Revolution. His talent as an artist and storyteller led him to the animation industry. Ronnie has contributed to many projects, including cowriting and codirecting *Inside Out*, the beloved Pixar film about big and small feelings that won the Academy Award for Best Animated Feature. In all of his work, Ronnie draws from his culture and experiences as a son and a father to create stories that bring families together.

# S. NEIL FUJITA

In 1941, Neil was a young art student when the US entered World War II following the Japanese attack on Pearl Harbor. He and over one hundred thousand Japanese Americans were treated with suspicion, forced to leave their homes and jobs, and incarcerated. Despite this injustice, Neil volunteered to serve in the US Army and joined the segregated 442nd Regimental Combat Team, the most decorated unit in American history. After the war, he returned to his art and created bold and modern designs for iconic books, album covers, and film posters. Neil is recognized as one of the most influential artists of his generation.

# WILLA KIM

Willa and Young-Oak were Korean American siblings who grew up in Southern California during the 1920s. Older sister Willa's artistic gifts and love of painting led to her dazzling career as a costume designer in the world of theater, dance, movies, and television. She created magnificent costumes, including marbled butterfly wings and glorious feather headpieces, and was well known for her pioneering work with painted stretch fabrics. Willa's creative and innovative costumes earned her much acclaim, including an Emmy Award and two Tony Awards.

# YOUNG-OAK KIM

Willa's brother, Young-Oak, was drafted into the US Army in 1941 after laws were changed to require all able-bodied men to register for the draft regardless of race. Young-Oak served in World War II with the 100th Infantry Battalion and the 442nd Regimental Combat Team, and again in the Korean War with the 31st Infantry Regiment. His bravery and leadership earned him nineteen medals. He retired as a colonel and one of the most decorated Asian American soldiers in US history. Young-Oak spent the rest of his life working as a humanitarian, helping lead Asian American communities in Southern California.

# DR. GRACE LEE BOGGS

As a young Chinese American woman, Grace experienced racism and struggled to find employment. When she witnessed Black Americans living in poor conditions similar to hers, she realized their struggles were connected. In the 1950s, Grace and her husband, James Boggs, became influential civil rights activists and community leaders in Detroit. For over seventy years, she dedicated herself to organizing, writing, protesting injustices, and advocating for a better future for working-class people. Grace once said, "If we want to see change in our lives, we have to change things ourselves."

# LYDIA X. Z. BROWN

Adopted from China as a baby by American parents, Lydia grew up in Massachusetts and was diagnosed with autism in middle school. Lydia felt pressure to keep their condition a secret from others, but that changed when they joined a disability rights organization as a teenager. They became empowered upon realizing that having autism just means that the brain works differently—it isn't something to hide or be ashamed of. Today, Lydia is an activist, educator, and attorney who fights to improve the lives of disabled and marginalized people.

# KRISTI YAMAGUCHI

Kristi made history in 1992 by becoming the first Asian American woman to win a gold medal at the Winter Olympic Games. As a young Japanese American girl growing up in California, Kristi watched figure skating at the age of six and knew she wanted to try it. She worked hard for many years to become a champion and has performed all around the world, captivating audiences with her grace and athleticism. Now Kristi is an author who advocates for childhood literacy through her Always Dream foundation.

# MICHELLE KWAN

Michelle has won the most medals of any figure skater in US history! The daughter of Chinese immigrants from Hong Kong, she first stepped on the ice at the age of five. As a young phenom, Michelle rocketed up the ranks and earned two Olympic medals, five world titles, and nine US titles. Through her skating, she has inspired countless people with her dedication and resilience. Today, Michelle bridges cultures and promotes positive values as a diplomat, with her most recent post as the US Ambassador to Belize.

# HINES WARD AND TROY POLAMALU

Hines was born in Seoul to Korean and Black parents. Troy, who is of Amer can Samoan descent, was born in California. While they came from different parts of the world, both discovered their destinies on the gridiron and became legendary players in the National Football League. As teammates, they led the Pittsburgh Steelers to many wins and two Super Bowl titles. Off the field, they are known for their kindness and generosity in helping others. Troy is recognized for his community service work, and Hines is admired for his anti-bullying advocacy.

# CONNIE CHUNG

Connie broke barriers as the first Asian person and only the second woman to anchor a newscast on a major American television network. Born in 1946 in Washington, DC, Connie was a quiet child in a large Chinese family but found her voice as a reporter. She overcame discrimination and bias by fearlessly pursuing important interviews with famous stars and world leaders. Connie has won three Emmy Awards and a Peabody Award for her work and changed people's perceptions of Asian American women, opening doors for future generations.

# PADMA LAKSHMI

Padma immigrated to America in 1974 when she was four years old. For many summers, she returned to India to visit her grandparents, who inspired her love of cooking and writing. She broke barriers as a supermodel and is now a bestselling author as well as an award-winning television personality and producer. In her work, Padma uses food to share stories, connect people, and highlight the beauty of different cultures. She is also an activist who draws on her own experiences to shine a light on those who are not always treated fairly, especially immigrants and women.

# DR. NARINDER SINGH KAPANY

Born in Punjab, India, in 1926, Narinder was a scientific pioneer who discovered that light can be bent and reflected. Known as "the father of fiber optics," he is regarded as one of the most important scientists of the twentieth century. Fiber optics are thin strands of glass and plastic that transmit data and information in the form of light. Internet, television, medical devices, and even toys use fiber optics! Dr. Kapany was also an educator, entrepreneur, and philanthropist who shared Sikh heritage, art, and culture to create better understanding.

# ISRAEL KAʻANOʻI KAMAKAWIWOʻOLE

Israel was born in 1959 on the island of Oʻahu surrounded by music. Invited to play on stage by performers at the Waikīkī music spot where his parents worked, IZ created magic with his uplifting voice and ʻukulele. Later, he formed a band called the Mākaha Sons. One of their songs, "Hawaiʻi ʻ78," protested the destruction of the island's natural beauty. Years later, his medley version of "Somewhere Over the Rainbow" and "What a Wonderful World" became a record-breaking global hit. Today, IZ is remembered for using his beautiful voice to share his culture and help his native community.

# STACEY PARK MILBERN

Born in 1987, Stacey was a queer Korean American woman with muscular dystrophy who became a disability and social justice activist. Understanding that disability is connected to other issues in society, she worked to uplift marginalized people. Sadly, Stacey passed away at the age of thirty-three, but the impact of her leadership is still felt today. In 2025, she was recognized on the US quarter for her compassionate work to create a world that everyone can participate in. Stacey once said, "I want to leave a legacy of disabled people knowing that we are powerful and beautiful because of who we are, not despite i⁻."

# EDITH KANAKA'OLE

Following the arrival of foreigners, Hawai'i's traditional culture was suppressed, and Native Hawaiians were discriminated against. "Aunty Edith" was a composer, oli chanter, and hula dancer who dedicated herself to keeping Native Hawaiian culture alive. With a beautiful lei po'o, or flower crown, on her head, Edith shared native traditions and history as a teacher and touring performer. In 1953, she opened her own hula school and helped develop a Hawaiian language program for students in the 1970s. In 2023, Edith was celebrated on the US quarter as an iconic leader in the Hawaiian Renaissance.

# JAWED KARIM AND STEVE CHEN

Steve and Jawed are part of the team that created YouTube, one of the world's most popular websites. Both immigrated to the US as kids—Steve was born in Taiwan and Jawed in Germany to a Bangladeshi father and a German mother. While they were gifted students, they took risks by leaving college early to join the California technology boom. There, they began working on a video-sharing website with their cofounder, Chad Hurley. YouTube launched in 2005, and today it has billions of visitors each month, impacting global events and the way that people share knowledge and information.

# OLIVIA RODRIGO

Olivia has always loved to perform. Growing up, she sang in talent competitions and acted in TV shows before focusing on music. In 2020, at the age of seventeen, Olivia wrote and recorded her hit debut single, "Drivers License." The song about heartbreak broke records, and her album *Sour* won many awards, launching her into superstardom. Olivia, whose father is Filipino American, connects with audiences of all ages but also uses her voice to speak out on important issues like women's rights. Though young, Olivia's impact continues to grow, just like her list of hit songs.

## MARK TATUM

Mark was born in Vietnam and grew up in Brooklyn with dreams of being a professional athlete. As a biracial kid in the 1970s, he faced bullying but overcame it with the support of his family. Although he decided to focus on his studies in college, Mark's determination still led him to a career in professional sports. He made history when he was unanimously appointed deputy commissioner and chief operating officer of the National Basketball Association in 2014. Today, Mark works to make basketball more inclusive for people everywhere.

## ERIK SPOELSTRA

Ever since he was a boy, Erik loved basketball. After playing the sport in high school and college, he received a life-changing opportunity to join the Miami Heat as a video coordinator. Erik's eye for the game propelled his impressive rise up the ranks, and in 2008, he became the first Filipino and Asian American head coach in the four major American sports leagues. Considered to be one of the greatest basketball coaches of all time, "Coach Spo" has led his teams to two NBA titles with an approach that is all about hard work, mental strength, and togetherness.

## LEE KIEFER

As children, the Filipino American Kiefer siblings cheered on their father in local fencing competitions. Lee and her brother and sister soon joined in, making fencing their family activity. Lee's fierce athleticism and determination helped her blaze a path to the international stage. At the 2020 Olympic Games, she became the first American fencer to win an individual foil gold medal. She went on to win two more gold medals at the 2024 Olympics. When she's not training and traveling around the world to compete, Lee is studying to become a doctor.

## IAN SEIDENFELD

When he was just seven years old, Ian began playing in the table tennis tournaments his Paralympic gold medalist father organized in Minnesota. Both father and son have a genetic condition called pseudoachondroplasia, which limits the growth of bones. Ian, whose mother is Chinese, worked very hard to master his intense style of play. At the 2020 Paralympic Games, Ian won the Class 6 gold medal in his Paralympic table tennis debut! Another medal was added to the family collection when he won bronze at the 2024 Paralympic Games.

# JANET YANG

Janet believes in the power of stories. When she started working as a producer in Hollywood, seeing true diversity on screen was rare, but that didn't stop her. Janet has produced many movies, including *The Joy Luck Club*, a groundbreaking story about Chinese American women. In 2022, she was elected President of the Academy of Motion Picture Arts and Sciences, making history as the first Asian American and only the fourth woman to hold the position. As a leader, Janet dedicates herself to uplifting underrepresented voices and promoting authenticity and inclusivity in the world of cinema.

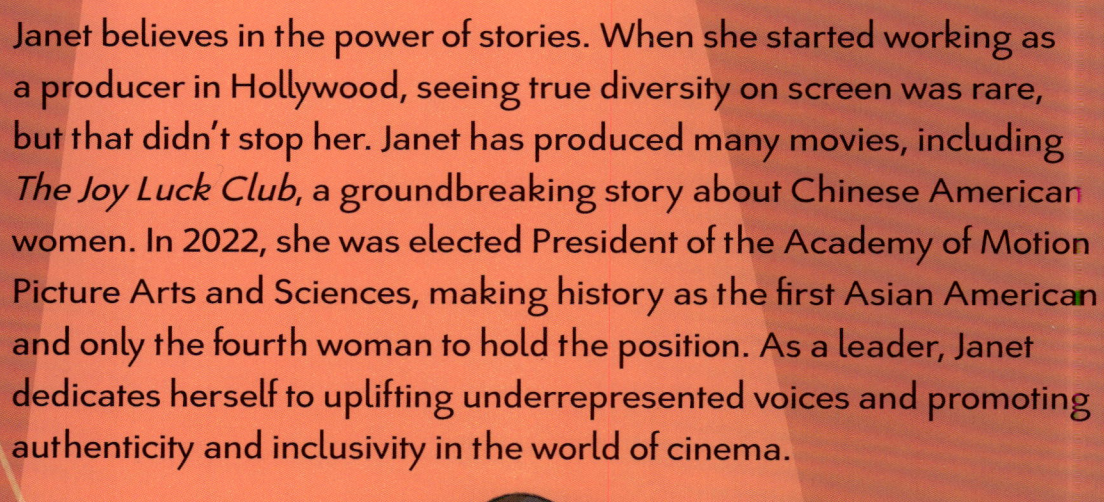

# KE HUY QUAN

When Ke was a young boy, his family escaped Vietnam and spent a year in a refugee camp before settling in the United States. At the age of twelve, he won life-changing roles in the iconic movies *Indiana Jones and the Temple of Doom* and *The Goonies*. However, following his early success, Ke struggled because there were few opportunities for Asian actors in Hollywood. After not acting for almost twenty years, he made a triumphant return in 2022 with his Academy Award–winning performance in *Everything Everywhere All at Once*. Ke's story of perseverance reminds people everywhere to keep believing in their dreams.

# FATIMA ALI

Fatima grew up in Pakistan and discovered her love of cooking at an early age. When she was eighteen years old, she immigrated to America for culinary school and later competed on *Chopped* and *Top Chef*. Chef Fati took pride in sharing her culture by introducing Pakistani flavors to her dishes. Just as her career was blossoming, Fatima was diagnosed with cancer. Before she passed away in 2019, she wrote about her hopes and her love of bringing joy to people. Fatima won two prestigious James Beard Foundation Awards for her writing and continues to inspire chefs today.

# CHRISTINE HA

Christine is a chef, restaurant owner, and disability advocate. Growing up, she loved her mother's delicious home-cooked Vietnamese food. When her mother passed away, Christine decided to teach herself how to cook and quickly discovered her love of serving others. Even after losing her eyesight due to a rare autoimmune disorder called neuromyelitis optica, she adapted and used her other senses to win the popular reality cooking show *MasterChef*. Today, Christine's spirit and success encourage people to do what they love, even if they have different abilities.

# ANDREW CHERNG AND PEGGY CHERNG

Andrew and Peggy were born in different countries but met at a small college in America. Both of Chinese descent, they opened the doors to the first Panda Express restaurant in a California mall in 1983. Together, the couple created a recipe for success thanks to their strong teamwork and love of helping people. Now you can find their Chinese-inspired food all over the world! To support local communities, Peggy and Andrew started the Panda Cares program to provide food, health care, and education to those in need. Giving back is important to the Cherngs. Andrew once said, "Life happens with help from other people."

# JHUMPA LAHIRI

As the daughter of a teacher and a librarian, Jhumpa had a natural love of books and reading. She often created stories as a child but was nervous to write as a grown-up until she was encouraged by her professor. Some of Jhumpa's stories reflect how difficult it is for her to be both Bengali and American when the two cultures are so different, a struggle that many immigrants share. Her debut book, *Interpreter of Maladies*, won the Pulitzer Prize for Fiction in 2000. Now, Jhumpa works as a writer, translator, and professor, encouraging her own students to read, write, and believe in themselves.

# OCEAN VUONG

Ocean fled Vietnam and came to America as a refugee when he was two years old. Despite struggling in school, he became the first person in his family to learn how to read or write well. Born Vinh Quoc Vuong, Ocean received his new name from his mother when she learned that "ocean" was the English word for the body of water that connects people and places. His love of words and passion for telling stories led him to become a brilliant poet who writes about the experience of being human. Today, Ocean is a bestselling and award-winning writer and teacher whose words inspire people around the world.

# AUTHORS' NOTE

We are filled with gratitude. It continues to be one of the greatest privileges of our lives to share the stories of incredible Asian Americans and Pacific Islanders.

While the impactful individuals highlighted in this book span different eras, backgrounds, and professions, they all believed in the power of their dreams. To our readers, be inspired! Live your lives with empathy, curiosity, and resilience so that you can overcome challenges and find happiness and fulfillment.

There is strength in commonality and community, but there is also tremendous value in learning from people with different experiences than our own. When we widen our perspectives and open our hearts and minds, we give ourselves the space to create a better, brighter, and more optimistic future. We humbly hope that this book can play a small role in helping us get there together.

Much love,
Maia and Alex